PENGUIN BOOKS

TWO WOMEN

Laurie Lee was born in Stroud, Gloucestershire, and educated at
Slad village school and at Stroud Central School. At the age
of nineteen he walked to London and then travelled on foot through
Spain where he was trapped by the outbreak of the Civil War –
to which he later returned by crossing the Pyrenees (as described in
his book *As I Walked Out One Midsummer Morning*).

He has published five books of poems: *The Sun My Monument* (1944),
The Bloom of Candles (1947), *My Many-Coated Man* (1955),
Pocket Poems (1960) and *Selected Poems* (1983). His other works include
a verse play for radio, *The Voyage of Magellan* (1948); a record
of his travels in Andalusia, *A Rose for Winter* (1955); his best-selling
autobiography, *Cider With Rosie* (1959); its
sequel *As I Walked Out One Midsummer Morning* (1969); and
I Can't Stay Long (1975).

Laurie Lee always wanted to be a painter but says he had difficulty
controlling his brushes.

TWO WOMEN

A Book of
Words and Photographs

LAURIE LEE

Penguin Books

Penguin Books Ltd, Harmondsworth, Middlesex, England
Viking Penguin Inc., 40 West 23rd Street, New York, New York 10010, U.S.A.
Penguin Books Australia Ltd, Ringwood, Victoria, Australia
Penguin Books Canada Ltd, 2801 John Street, Markham, Ontario, Canada L3R 1B4
Penguin Books (N.Z.) Ltd, 182–190 Wairau Road, Auckland 10, New Zealand

First published by André Deutsch 1983
Published in Penguin Books 1984

Made and printed in Great Britain by
William Collins & Co. Ltd.,
Glasgow

To My Family

My thanks are due to The Hogarth Press Ltd for kindly
allowing me to reprint an amended extract from my essay
THE FIRSTBORN which they first published in 1964.

My photographs in this book are of the two women who have occupied most of my late adult life, enclosing it in a double embrace, like bookends.

I met the first one in the village of Martigues, in Provence, while on my way to the Pyrenees. She was a stumpy, wriggly, golden-curled little girl of five, and spoke a slurred incomprehensible French dialect. Her mother was English, her father a blond French fisherman, himself the son of a Swedish sea-captain who had briefly stopped off at Marseilles.

The day of our autumn meeting, in her mother's garden above the lake, the father was down in the port drinking *pastis* with friends. I remember the child sitting on my lap, squirming her plump body against me and looking up at me with brilliant slit eyes of squinting blue. As she licked the sugar of a bun from her fat pink lips, she studied me with intense regard. I don't know who she thought I was – this crumpled twenty-two-year-old English stranger – but it was then, she swears, she decided to marry me.

That meeting was brief and speechless, and I'm still enchanted by her random choice, though even now I don't understand it. Was it because I was a couple of inches taller than most of the blue-chinned fishermen in her village, shorter than her father, yet blond like him?

She has never made this clear, only her determination at the time. But I remember still that round, rosy, squeezed-up face; the abundant uncared-for curls, and chiefly the diamond brilliance of her unclouded eyes.

We spent the afternoon in that mute, rather

lopsided communion, under the autumn shade of a mulberry tree. Then her handsome father came home, and with a grunt she switched laps: and I went on to Spain, and forgot her for a while.

When next I saw her, some few years later, she was striding down the Kings Road, Chelsea; nubile, arms swinging, straight and tall, her limbs clad in a tight blue frock; her large eyes steady, though unfocussed, on the way ahead, and on the soldiers who assailed her with their grubby glances. She must have been about thirteen at the time, sturdily curved and comely. She always said she developed early.

Her father had been tragically killed in the war, and after the German Occupation her mother had brought her to England. They were staying with an aunt in that handsome row of terraced houses which has since become Chelsea Fire Station.

Though the girl was changed and twice-grown from the chubby child I'd first dandled in Martigues, I recognized her immediately; the frisky lights in her hair – though it was now less a curled halo than a heavy gold fall on her shoulders; the animal charm of her movements, the blind swagger of her walk, but most of all the slashing blue of her eyes.

She had with her, on that occasion, two slightly older girl-cousins, each of them of heart-stopping beauty, jet dark as she was fair, nervous but assured, and agile and mischievous at times as lemurs. As she strode down the road, the two slim frisky creatures teased and looped and circled around her, but she went on her way, her shoulders back, seemingly unaware of their affectionate malice.

She was not unaware of me, however, as she made clear enough when I called on her aunt soon after. I had known the aunt for some time and occasionally visited her house in the evenings where I might find a few painters and musicians gathered. The girl-cousins would be allowed to stay up and enjoy the flow of intellectual nourishment. Cathy, being that much younger, was sent to bed.

When she went, unprotesting, she'd take my overcoat from the hall and hang it on the inside of

her bedroom door. Later, when it was time for me to leave, I had always to enter that snug little trap upstairs, where she'd slip drowsily from her bed in a shower of crumpled cotton and help me into my coat with many innocent pressures of hand and thigh. 'I don't know anything about Strindberg,' she'd say, giving me that trusting niece-to-uncle look.

In due course Cathy's widowed mother married a charming old Italian professor, and they all went to live in a little house in Kensington. It was towards the end of the war, and London was short of men, and being one of the few of them I was spoilt indeed; but Cathy in the evenings – all schoolgirl blouses and ribbons – became for me a regular rest and a refuge.

Together we'd wander Kensington's deserted back-gardens, knee-deep in weeds and unpruned roses, walking free and silent through the bomb-broken mansions, the littered ballrooms and snapped-off stairways leading to rising moons and displaced owls. Hot, scented twilights of war-end summer. I was not even required to discuss her homework. I'd lead her here and there, then we'd go burrowing down into some dead servant's cellars and I'd know the sudden strength of her sixth-form arms.

As soon as the war ended, and Europe re-opened, Cathy's mother wished to take her back to Martigues for a visit; and as their acknowledged but ambiguous protector I, of course, was asked to go with them. We took cartons of cigarettes, tins of coffee, and soap, and cranked slowly by train through a land of smashed towns and bridges, and fields dotted with the shells of tanks.

A small tin of Lyons coffee paid for three nights in a Paris hotel, and fifty cigarettes for our food and drink. I remember the thin, bitter faces of the Parisians still, and their fawning hatred as we settled our bills.

Then we were back in Martigues, in the unstained sunlight of that place, and Cathy was home again. Not so her poor mother, who was still the foreigner who had married the town's drowned hero. It seemed that the villa by the lakeside, where I'd first met Cathy, had passed into cleverer hands. Cathy's huge seventy-year-old grandmother couldn't put us up; she was living in a one-room shack with her lover. So we stayed with a tight-lipped neighbour in a small-holding just outside the town. Mother and

daughter slept in the stable, and I in the loft above.

But gathering later down in the port, Cathy unlocked all emotions. Her smiling youth, her beauty, and vague russet charm, returned to the hearts of all who had known her. Old women, like bent monkeys, ran across the dazzling streets to embrace her. Old and young fisherman gulped down their glasses of *pastis* and stumbled out onto the pavements to kiss her cool young cheeks. 'Katie! Katie! No, it's not possible – a miracle. *Si belle, si belle! Et tout comme sa père – le pauvre, le pauvre . . .*'

Tears were shed, both for Cathy and her return, and for the memory of her father whose face and presence seemed restored by hers. Men

and women, squat little school-children in aprons, the huge waddling grandmother, the many dwarf-like cousins, they stroked and prodded her, touching her hair and shoulders, surrounding her with their amazed exclamations, while she just stood patiently among them in a mist of pleased misunderstanding and smiled her dazzling smile.

Cathy was about fourteen now, and I saw what her visit must have meant to the village, a resurrection of youth and a reassurance. I think it was then, perhaps for the first time, that I truly noticed Cathy's clear gold beauty, and the depth of her eyes, huge as picture windows. They were of an extraordinary stretched blue and reflected all the vast vacancy of the heavens. She also had her lost father's strength, and simplicity of nature. She had no guile or suspicion of treachery.

When we returned to England Cathy went back to finish her schooling – a red-striped blazer-girl from Parson's Green High. By the time she was fifteen I was taking her on trips to the seaside. A Wilson-Steer child in a blue dress wading thigh-deep in the waves. Roundabouts, fish and chips, and popcorn. She, lightly leaning against me, smiling and listening, saying nothing. Then to the well-scrubbed guest-house in a Hastings backstreet, separate rooms, and the whisper of bare feet in the night.

Not till she finally left school did she first mention marriage. Just in passing. 'I'd be no trouble,' she said. I was now over thirty, a known bachelor, and had always turned my face from such engagements. Sometimes I used to dream that I was, in fact, married and I'd wake up with a violent start. I needed the company of women more than I needed the company of men, but I required isolation even more.

I had known this lovely girl for several years now, steering and leading her through her adolescence. Her mother seemed to have accepted my role of instructor and pathfinder and gave us unusual freedom; but as soon as Cathy reached seventeen, and nothing had been positively declared between us, the mother snapped into action, swept her daughter off to Florence, and left me to concentrate my mind.

A ploy that seldom fails. Cathy was away eight months and didn't write, though she sent me some smoked cheese for Christmas. My bachelor's room in Chelsea had grown greyer and more barren, and the intimations of a sterile death moved upon me. I also missed the presence of that acquiescent and radiant girl who seemed to care for no other company but mine. In the spring I telegraphed her mother the no doubt expected message. 'Please send Cathy back. I'd like to marry her.' The girl was still legally under-age, but both she – and a signed certificate of parental consent to the marriage – were speedily furnished as soon as I'd cabled the fare.

Cathy had left for Florence the previous summer, a shapely, tight-limbed, flat-bellied young beauty, but when I met her at Victoria, after her eight months of spaghetti and idleness, I quickly spotted the physical difference. More radiant than ever, she seemed twice the size, as though specially plumped up for a Pasha. I led her to a station weighing-machine and put in a penny. 'If you're over twelve stone,' I said, 'you're going straight back to your mother.' She passed the test by a couple of ounces.

She was now in my hands and care, as she has been ever since. We took a small Earl's Court flat overlooking the railway. Her cooking was primitive, and we both lost weight. But her presence now was one of constant beauty and quietness. Living with her was like living by a pool of heavenly reflections, a gentle ruffling and resettling of light. She also looked after me with a sort of ardent amateurishness of purpose, not so much anticipating my needs as stumbling prettily along close after.

Then came the May morning which she announced was the day of our wedding. Although never a great organizer, being somewhat forgetful, she'd fixed, without my knowing, the licence at the Kensington Register Office, together with the date and the time.

As we left for the ceremony her long hair had never looked more rich and abundant, and was crimped with a kind of Earl's Court ripple; and her eyes that morning shone with a mysterious double radiance which I've only once seen equalled since, when she won an electric steam-iron on the stage of the Walham Green Empire.

But seldom has a straight-backed child-bride gone off to her wedding attended by less extravagance or fuss. No motorcar, special clothes, crowding guests or cameras; just a few ribbons in her summer dress. We walked up to Barkers, where I bought her a spray of lilies of the valley, then on to the Register Office and a ceremony of official curtness. (I was nervous and the Registrar suddenly broke off to remind me that this was a solemn occasion and would I kindly stop sucking sweets?)

Afterwards we had champagne in a Kensington High Street pub, then went on to a Soho restaurant I knew. 'We've just got married,' I said. A shudder of occasion ran up the head waiter's body. He gave us a secluded table and loaded it with food and wine. 'Today you don't pay,' he said heavily, suggesting that the future would take care of the reckoning. As word got round, other waiters gathered in moony groups in the distance, heads tilted, eyes soft and moist as they looked at Cathy, sharp as knives when they looked at me. The luncheon was long, sumptuous, proud and wordless. Just we two, no guests, except for an old sepia photograph of my Mother which we'd propped against an empty glass.

I remember little else of that wedding feast, or of what we ate or drank. Cathy sat smiling at no one in particular, was for the most part happily silent, or squirmed and sighed gently from time to time and glanced sideways at the distantly attentive waiters. They left us alone, except to give her little jerky bows. They knew, and she knew, that she was the queen of that moment.

I went woozily back to work that afternoon, and in the evening we had rabbit stew. So began our married life in the Earl's Court flat — two furnished rooms and a screened-off kitchen. Otherwise we had nothing. Cathy sent me off in the mornings with curiously wrapped sandwiches, sometimes with the fillings forgotten, or the margarine spread on the outside. It was a play-acting time, Cathy was too young to know what marriage demanded and me too old to take it seriously. But not too old to know that I had an extraordinary beauty on my hands and that she had quietly occupied my life.

Presently we moved to a flat in Elm Park Gardens, and I left my job and decided to live by writing. We had little enough in the Earl's Court days. Now we had even less. Bare rooms, a borrowed bed, basins of plain boiled spaghetti. We began to put on weight again. I don't know if Cathy realized how poor we were then. I never heard her mention it.

At that time the tall kipper-coloured houses in Elm Park Gardens, were mostly occupied by families from the bombed London docks. Gaunt worried mothers sat out on the doorsteps; bantam-cock fathers strutted off to the pubs. The empty roads and gardens were taken over by graceful gangs of grubby children to whom these spaces became their exclusive playgrounds. Secret hopping games possessed the pavements, accompanied by inscrutable chanting. Complex lines and patterns, as old as the Chaldees, were chalked boldly across the streets. The motorcar had yet to take over. This was still the children's free kingdom. Their cries of celebration and battle enlivened the air.

On summer afternoons, Cathy and I often had tea in the garden, surrounded by this curious and enquiring brood. The girls stood on their heads, showing off their knickers, then shared our broken biscuits. 'You a hundred yet?' one of them would say, gazing closely into my baggy eyes. Then, as Cathy carried the tea-things back into the flat: 'Mr Lee, aren't you lonely living in there – you know, just you and your mum?'

Then, with the coming of the money-making middle-fifties, Elm Park Gardens were tidied up. The bombed families were removed and filed away out of sight in the council's new flats in World's End. Their places were taken by rows of kerb-hugging motorcars and a few tiny snapping dogs.

Cathy missed the children and was as aware as I was of the new affluent silence surrounding us. I worked all day in my little back room, and at tea-time she brought me pigs' liver on toast. I was publishing very little and we were living on about £200 a year. Luckily, richer young friends frequently asked us to supper. Recently married, like us, but living in small pretty houses, newly furnished and decorated, with plush drawing-rooms, coal fires and candlelit dining-rooms, and nursery cots already crammed overhead.

Those long 1950s were barren for Cathy, try as she might to keep it from me. There was a loving emptiness about her; also a sense of heavy drowsed waiting as of a shadowed fruit-tree in bud, but spellbound. Not overtly religious, she'd rigged up a secret altar for herself in an odd corner of an unused passage. She'd covered a galvanized coal-bin with a shawl, and decorated it with candles and a small crucifix. Sometimes I'd catch a glimpse of her kneeling at the coal-bin and praying. Why and to whom, I could only guess.

So we lived on in our flat, quietly through her early twenties, while she grew ever more beautiful, her skin riper, yet cool, her hair longer, lighter, her flawless eyes waiting for reflections and explanations which, perhaps fortunately, never came.

I also remember the locked-up London feeling we shared at that time – moons glimpsed only occasionally through the city's gaseous sky-glow, the seasons cranking themselves irrelevantly over the roof-tops: sooty frost on the window-boxes, spring grass pushing through pavements, then booming summer rolling in with its huge gold evenings, leading to the wet fall of autumn, freezing November mists and the feeling of a year passed and paid for without experience.

I'd always wished one day to return to that Gloucestershire village I'd grown up in, but I knew that this would require cash and cunning. I'd walked out twenty-odd years earlier, to seek the world and fortune, a difficult and unpopular thing to do, and if one returned at all it was best not to return a beggar.

Shut up with Cathy in the London top-floor flat, gazing out together at the blue-smudged skies, the need to go back west grew steadily stronger; I was well on in my thirties, and messages from my home landscape seemed to drift in on every wind. That was a place where every tree and hedge and hill and stone, had for me a deeper meaning than any other seen elsewhere. I explained this to Cathy, and she said; 'O.K.,' and gave me more liver on toast.

Then suddenly, unexpectedly, something happened which changed our lives for good. I published a book which went to the top of the charts, and all kinds of luck seemed to attend its launching. It was due out in June, a sleepy time for bookselling, but a printers' and binders' strike held it up. All forthcoming books were stacked in a queue, and by chance mine stood at the head. When the strike was settled, just before Christmas, my book, together with Pope-Hennessy's *Life of Queen Mary*, were the only ones to be found in the shops. When it came to buying Christmas presents, even at Harrods, there was nothing to be had save Pope-Hennessy and me, and and perhaps a few decorative jars of bath-salts.

It seemed that *Cider with Rosie* was being bought not singly but in bundles, and overnight Cathy and I were rich. From scraping along on £200 a year, we were now getting huge cheques from the publishers. We went off to Paris for a winter weekend, and found a hotel of extreme elegance overlooking the Quai d'Orsay, and Cathy wore things she had never worn before, and the dry years melted in her eyes, and her native French came back to her with a flow of warmth and excitement like living breath to a neglected flute.

Back in London we relished the oddness of success – strangers invited us, old friends avoided us, Cathy bought meat every day, and a few more new clothes, and now there was always a bottle of Scotch in the house.

More important than this, we were no longer imprisoned by London and poverty, and soon found a cottage in the country. It was stone-built, stone-tiled, with a long raftered attic, small angled windows set in deep stone walls, low ceilings, heavy doors, a Victorian range, and an outdoor tap and lavatory. It was a snug little fortress built when country-folk had no wish for views or picture-windows, merely a refuge from the open air.

Inevitably, I suppose, and even more fateful-ly, the cottage was stuck right in the middle of the village I'd grown up in; a few steps from the pub, the church, the school, the post office, and the place where the old carter used to pick up his parcels.

This was the village I'd written about in *Cider with Rosie*, and some of my old neighbours were quite fidgety to see me back. But Cathy made it easier, having clearly had no part in it, while her youth and beauty were the subject of charmed speculation.

Throughout over twenty years of exile, this cluster of unkempt houses, set in its deep green valley, had filled my nights with vivid and recurring dreams. Now I'd come home again, and felt I'd never left it – the damp stones and moss and brilliant fields, the church bell and lace-white faces at the windows – all were unchanged, even the familiar temperature of the rain and the blackbird singing away in his local accent.

I think that Cathy, displaced as she had so often been, felt that this could also be her home. We kept on the London flat; it was where I worked most easily; but the cottage was going to take up much of our lives. We moved in in the autumn, and I returned to boyhood, gathering and cutting wood.

The Victorian range soon crackled with beech-twigs and pine-cones, and washing steamed in front of it as in the days of my Mother. Cathy began to clear the garden. She burnt old leaves and wore a special hat. She seemed to be making a nest, but she also stood for long minutes at a time just gazing at the ground or out across the valley.

I think I remember her most clearly, during those first days at the cottage, as someone who felt herself locked out, a wistful fugitive, peering in through the windows as though seeking to be admitted; eyes large and questioning, still wondering who she was, where and to whom she most truly belonged.

True, we'd been married twelve years now, boxed-up in sterile London, with her ripe golden self still inexplicably childless. Now I'd brought her back to my beginnings, to the place where I was born and formed, a re-starting and starting ground for us both.

When it happened, by what magic did it come about? What spell had been preserved here for us? Was it the angle of the light, the special dew in the stones, the local pitch of birdsong, the close thrust of the hills? What was it, after twelve years, that finally loosed the knot, set the seed, and worked the miracle?

I still don't know. But one morning I walked into the kitchen and found Cathy perched up on the window-sill. She looked at me transfigured, her eyes full of confusion and triumph.

'Oh, Lol!' she said. 'Would you believe it? . . . I'm pregnant.' And she slipped into my arms and wept.

Cathy was never one for old wives' tales, and continued to live the life she always had — abstractedly active, pushing and heaving her way through domestic muddles and quite forgetting at times what was happening to her. Then again there were days when she'd sit for a long time motionless as though wondering whether this late visitation was real.

In early spring I had to go to Mexico for a magazine, and while there I noticed the corn-dollies, crucifixes and fertility sheaves of maize stalks which many Indian villagers nailed to their rooftops. They so much resembled those I'd seen made in the Cotswolds that I brought a boxful back home.

I was only away for a couple of weeks, but when I returned I found Cathy in bed with a threatened miscarriage. Sublimely unaware of what not to do in her condition, she'd been moving the furniture, and painting the cottage ceilings, and pushing great stones round the garden.

Cathy was over thirty now, and four months pregnant, and didn't know what risks she'd been running. 'Yes, it's possible she could lose it,' the doctor said; meanwhile she must just lay quiet.

Cathy had never been ill before. She was the one who visited the sick, whisked up medicines and carried comforts to others. Now she lay pale and beautiful, like a blaached Botticelli, stretched in her great brass bed, and apologizing. After years of unthinking ministrations to others, it was she who now lay weak and wounded, it was she to whom the neighbours were now bringing soup and comforts, and she just couldn't understand it.

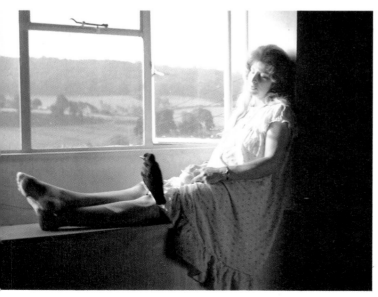

A great chill hung over the cottage, a cloud of doubt, a feeling of being cheated at the last moment of hope. Better no hope at all than this; I didn't want another of life's little ironies – at least not where Cathy was concerned. She'd always been of such an ungrumbling innocence she could go out into a hailstorm, raise her face to the sky, and never know what hit her.

On the first night of my return, when Cathy was asleep, I slipped a box of Mexican corn-dolls under her bed. I reckoned we needed the help of any gods we could gather. But Cathy was strong, and perhaps protected by her nature from the blasphemy of such a late betrayal. Gradually she recovered and took over the cottage again; summer came, and she grew more radiant with the lengthening days. The doctor said he was surprised, but always thought she'd be all right. At least, that's what he said he thought.

With the danger past, a new light shone in Cathy's face, maybe explained by the many sources of her extraordinary beauty – French, Italian, Irish, Swedish, German, Jewish, Scots – all gathered in one celebration. It was something I'd not seen so clearly before. As though calling on the spirits of her ancestors, she settled down to wait.

Then the mysterious visitors began to arrive: the first, an exhausted pigeon. He flopped down on the doorstep one early morning, trailed his wings and hobbled inside and crawled under the kitchen table. There he plumped himself out, his eyes split with sleep, roosted and made the place home.

He stayed under the table for well over a

week, wrapped in a blue breathing puff of slumber. Cathy put down saucers of grain and water, which he seemed to ignore, but which disappeared in the night. We grew used to this twitching lump under our table, but wondered why he'd chosen us for his refuge.

Then one morning, just before dawn, we were awakened by a series of flustered rustlings on the stairs, vigorous flappings interspersed with silence; then into the bedroom appeared our resurrected pigeon, eyes bright, head swivelling, toes lightly spread, looking for some dimly remembered loft.

Cathy loved that bird, cradled and nourished him, and as he grew stronger he still stuck to the house. I'd see him everywhere, waddling around like a lodger, perched on chairs, on the mantelpiece, on the tops of clocks, or shadowing Cathy out to the kitchen. With rest and care he had become restored, cocky, his coo bubbling and fresh, his body blue and sharp as a bullet.

But the day came at last when he strode out into the garden, peered about him, then flew up to the rooftop. He roosted there for a couple of days and neither grain nor calling would bring him down. He just shuffled to and fro, looking out over the valley and focussing on ever enlarging distances. Were we simply a staging post, Cathy wondered, or had he brought us some message? When he suddenly flew off and left us, she wept.

He had not gone long, however, when a jackdaw took over, almost as though by arrangement. Another dawn arrival, he came swooping down out of the beechwoods with a rousing cry, straight through the window and onto the bedpost. We'd just woken up to find him perching there, clearing his throat with a kind of throttling cackle. Then he stretched his wings wide, folded them cloakwise around him, and eyed us like a turbulent priest.

We got up immediately, of course, and the jackdaw took over, occupying the house, our lives, our days and nights, or swooping watchfully from tree to tree around us. Aggressive, always hungry, thrusting and demanding, he settled in and looked like staying for ever.

Was he also, I wondered, a shadow cast before us? He used to ride about on Cathy's head and shoulders. He constantly bothered her for food, and if he didn't get it he'd bite her ear with a beak like tweezers. Sometimes he'd fly back up to the beechwoods, but even there he still seemed to manage to keep his black eyes on us. If he was out of our sight, we were still in his. A call from Cathy at the window, and he would answer with a croak of impatient affection, then return in slow gliding swoops across the corner of the valley, to perch on her shoulder and begin worrying her hair.

It was late summer now, and Cathy's time had nearly arrived, although she said she couldn't be sure. She used to sit in the garden shelling peas and beans and the afternoon sun lifted a luminous glow to her cheeks. The jackdaw crouched nearby, croaking to be fed, or sleeping. Cathy, in her loose blue gown, now had a look of magnified beauty, and a haunting, invalid pallor. Her normally rose cheeks had beneath their skin a chilling light as from the far recess of a rockpool.

In the gold mornings of September, when she was now at her heaviest, she used to go with the jackdaw up to the attic. I'd see her heaving herself up in a billow of blue and white with this scampering black dart behind her. She'd take a saucer of milk and stretch herself out on the window-sill, and the jackdaw would sit on her naked feet. Then, after some preliminary chattering and fluttering of feathers, he'd move up and perch on her knee. Cathy would dip her finger in the milk and hold it out, and his beak would enclose it with a clattering passion, thrusting and sucking with the power of a hawk while angry thrills ran through his outspread wings.

Seeing them both together – the billowing blue-and-gold girl and her frenzied black-beaked companion – they seemed already to have come to an understanding. She was the one from whom all blessings flowed, and he, for all his ranting and bullying, affectionately knew it.

The jackdaw stayed with Cathy throughout most of that September, then one day, like the pigeon, he went. Calling his name brought no sign or answering call from the beechwoods. Again, like the pigeon, he seemed to have delivered his message.

Mornings and evenings were darker now, the garden more loaded with the late light of summer. Sunflowers and nasturtium, in one last daze of colour, began to break and cast their seeds. Cathy moved about with a honey-coated slowness like a great bee that had lost its bearings, fumbling and stumbling and bumping into things, and muttering drily under her breath. Pigeon and jackdaw were gone, the child only a skin away; we were alone together for perhaps the last time in our lives.

Cathy was restless, sleeping badly, so I

moved to the little room next to hers. One night I heard her pacing the floor, opening and closing windows, and uttering little muffled groans. The oil-lamp was lit, and her face was white and sweating. 'Is this it?' 'No, no,' she was holding her stomach and shaking her head. 'Just something I ate. Don't worry.'

She went back to bed but was soon pacing the floor again. Her groans were more frequent now. It was nearly dawn, and her bedsheets were soaking wet. 'My hot water bottle's leaking.' She groaned again. 'Nothing to bother about. I'll be all right in the morning.'

I dressed and called the neighbours, who drove us to the Maternity Hospital, while Cathy gasped and giggled and said it couldn't be for a long time yet. When we arrived, the Matron – my cousin Marion – looked at Cathy, then turned on me. 'What happened then Laurie? You daft or something? You should have brought her here hours ago.'

I went home, having been told to telephone later I stirred Cathy's plum-wine a couple of times, hung about, cut some wood, then climbed the bank and telephoned from the call-box, but was told to have patience, there was no news yet. So I settled down at the kitchen table to work on an article about Holland; and towards the middle of the afternoon, describing the curious, shut-tered, puritan village of Staphorst, I recalled a young girl I'd seen there, standing alone in her Sunday garden, and I found myself writing; '. . . born to this village, and perhaps never to leave it.' And at that sentence I stopped, and knew I needn't wait any longer. I climbed back to the call-box and telephoned again.

Matron was some time in coming, then I heard her brisk footsteps down the corridor. 'That you, Laurie? You got a daughter.' As quick and easy as that; no build-up.

The kiosk is on the steep bank above the cottage, and its glass walls command the length of the valley. I held the telephone in silence, looking out over the golden woods, thinking: you've got a daughter; they couldn't be wrong about that, could they? What you wanted above all things in the world. As I stood there I felt my life returning at last, and my daughter's stretching out before me.

Then I heard a sharp voice at the other end of the telephone. 'Laurie? What's the matter with you? Dropped dead or something? You better hurry on round. They're waiting to see you.' So I went, and found mother and child in bed together. Cathy met me with an exultant smile of divided love.

This then was my daughter, born in the autumn and a late fall into my life, lying purple and dented like a little bruised plum, as though she'd been lightly trodden in the grass and forgotten.

Then the Matron picked her up and she came suddenly alive, her bent legs kicking crabwise, and the first living gesture I saw was a thin wringing of the hands accompanied by a far-out Hebridean lament.

This moment of meeting seemed to be a birthtime for both of us; her first and my second life. Nothing, I knew, could ever be the same again, and I think I was reasonably shaken. I peered intently at her, looking for familiar signs, but she was as convulsed as an Aztec idol. Was this really my daughter, this purple concentration of grief, this blind and protesting dwarf?

Then they handed her to me, stiff and howling, and I held her for the first time and kissed her, and she went still and quiet as though by instinctive guile, and I was instantly enslaved by her flattery of my powers.

Newborn, of course, she looked already a centenarian, tottering on the brink of an old crone's grave, exhausted, shrunken, bald as Voltaire, mopping, mowing, and twisting wrinkled claws in speechless spasms of querulous doom.

But with each day of survival, once her mother had brought her home, she grew younger and fatter, her face drawing on life, every breath of real air healing the birth-death stain she had worn so witheringly at the beginning.

This girl then, my child, this parcel of will

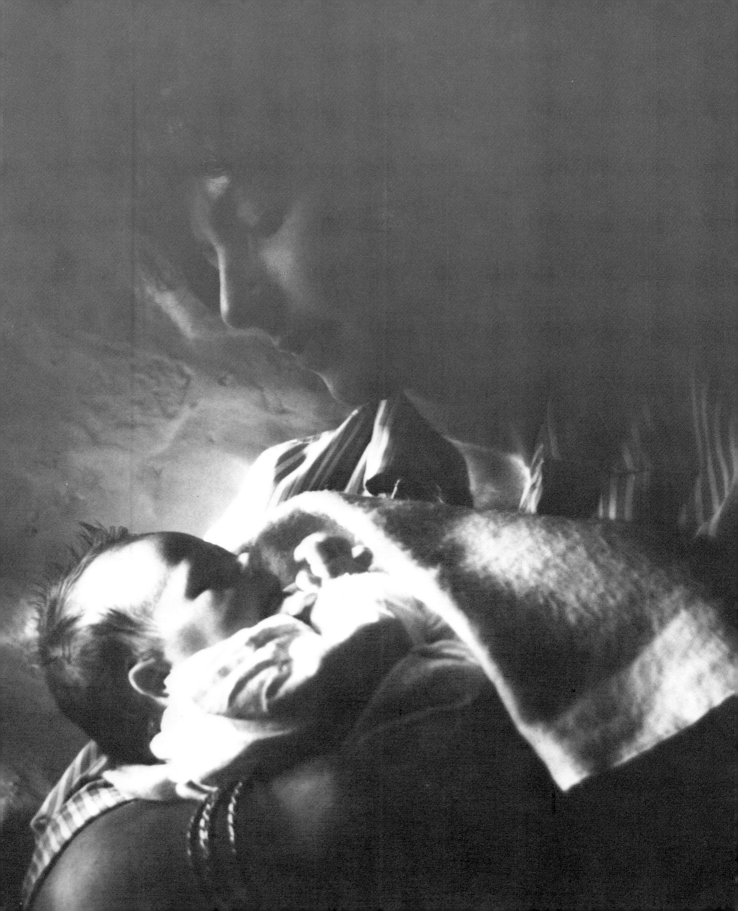

and warmth, began to fill the cottage with her obsessive purpose. The rhythmic tides of her sleeping and feeding spaciously measured our days and nights. Her frail absorption was a commanding presence, her helplessness strong as a rock, so that I found myself listening even to her silences as though some great engine was purring upstairs.

When awake, and not feeding, she'd give dry snorts and gobbles, very like our departed jackdaw; or strain and groan and wave her hands about as though casting invisible nets.

As I watched her at this I saw her hauling on life, groping fiercely with every limb and muscle, working blind at a task no one could properly share, in a darkness where she was still alone.

She was of course just an ordinary miracle, but was also the particular late wonder of my life. So almost every night, at first, I'd take her to bed like a book and lie close and study her. Her dark blue eyes would stare straight into mine, but off-centre, not seeing me.

Such moments could have been the best we would ever know, those midnights of mutual blindness, while I was safe from her first recognitions, and she'd stare idly through me, at the pillow, at the bedhead, at the light on the wall, and each was a shadow of indifferent importance.

Here she was then, my daughter, here, alive, the one I must possess and guard. A year before this space had been empty, not even a hope of her was in it. Now she was here, brand new, with our name upon her, and no one could call in the night to reclaim her.

She was here for good, her life stretching before us, and so new I couldn't leave her alone.

She was a time-killing lump, her face a sheaf of masks which she'd shuffle through aimlessly. One by one she'd reveal them, while I watched eerie rehearsals of those emotions she would one day need; random, out-of-sequence, but already exact, automatic but strangely knowing – a quick pucker of fury, a puff of ho-hum boredom, a beaming after-dinner smile, perplexity, slyness, a sudden wrinkling of grief, pop-eyed interest, and fat-lipped love.

I'd been handed twenty-odd years wrapped up in this bundle, and hoped to see her grow, learn to totter, to run into the garden, run back, and call this place home. But I realized from these beginnings that I'd got a daughter whose life was

already separate from mine, whose will already followed its own directions, and who was quickly correcting my woolly preconceptions of her by being something quite different. She was a child of herself and would be what she was, I was merely the keeper of her temporary helplessness.

But for the rest, I hoped she might be my own salvation, for any man's child is his second chance. In this role I saw her leading me back to my beginnings, re-opening rooms I'd locked and forgotten, stirring the dust in my mind by asking the big questions – as any child could do.

But in my case, perhaps, just not too late; she was already persuading me that there might yet be time, that with her, my tardy but bright-eyed

pathfinder, I might return to that wood which long ago I fled from, but which together we might enter and know.

I looked closely and carefully at what was before me now. After those twelve years with only the presence of Cathy in my life, the constant rose-glow of her beauty like an unabating summer, I had now this other one, sunk deep in her wicker cradle, huffing, puffing, grumbling and snoring, unknown, unpredictable, fragile and alien, yet already a third power whose strength I could only guess at, but who was working up steam to take over her huge part of our lives.

Mother and daughter were at home, enclosed in the warm cottage walls, the winter sun lighting up their nuzzling faces, and I'd see them clinging, heads together, wrapped in their secret needs, continually trying out new arrangements and harmonies.

But I was not shut out. I was the watcher, and they were twin stars circling each other in mutual orbit. So I watched them continuously in their changing phases – the child in the evening carried round like a candle illuminating her mother's face, or curled against her in the morning, half-dazed with sleep, in the cool brightness of the cottage kitchen.

The two seemed as alike as clouds, lustrously bobbing together and physically a part of the same moving weather. They also lay around for hours in a kind of besotted idleness, while the child fed on her mother with little running kisses, exploring lips and hair with quick crawling fingers. But she was moved to panic if the mother slept, clambering over her body with anxious

whispers, trying to prod and breathe her back into life. When the mother stirred and awoke, there were urgent outbursts of love, loud cries, and squeals, and hugs of welcome, as though each had returned separately from a distant country. I think the child really believed that she had worked the resurrection, that her warmth and kisses had caused the miracle.

Of course it was not always like this. Mother and child quarrelled from the beginning, each possessing parallel but divergent wills. Like sister-ships they were hauled together in the same emotional estuary while riding strong and contrary currents. I suppose this to be the fate of nearly all parents: mothers and daughters share the same prison cells, meshed in rival jealousies and irritations; while fathers, hoping to be their daughters' liberators, double-lock them with silken keys.

But I like to remember the two in the lamplit evenings by the cottage fire, during the first of those newborn weeks, the child feeding at the breast, the sleepy adjusting fingers, the bunting mouth, the little grunts of concentration and bliss. I don't think I've ever seen them since in such a state of single-minded agreement, so quietly immersed in their shared purposes.

At these moments I often used to play a Schubert record on the gramophone – a slow movement from one of his trios – hoping that such deep beauty and calm might be absorbed by the child and mixed with her life's original nourish-

ment. A sloppy and fanciful idea, no doubt; I still wonder if it made any difference.

Jessy we called her, and she grew quickly from her first bruised softness to a sturdy, curly-haired beauty, a Pears'-soap angel with a sharp sting of carbolic, a thing of surging and unknowable forces. Had Cathy, in the long stillness and abstraction of her twelve married years, known she had been waiting for this? For all the first overcoatings of sentimental expectations, Jessy soon proved to be a paint-stripping reality, and Cathy welcomed and embraced her like a demon lover.

As she grew and changed, I was increasingly wondering what this new girl could be, with her ecstatic adorations and rages. The beaming knife-keen awakening, cracking the dawn like an egg, her furies at the small frets of living, the long fat slumbers, almost continental in their reaches, the bedtimes of chuckles, private jokes and languors.

And who was I to her? The rough dark shadow of pummelling games and shouts, the cosy frightener, the tossing and swinging arms, lifting the body to the highest point of hysteria before lowering it back again to the safe male smell.

But she was my girl now, the second force in my life, and with her puffed, knowing eyes, forever moving with colour and light, she was well aware of it.

Her manipulations of me began before she could speak, and I was too fond to withstand them. Lying on a coloured blanket in the morning, rigid with expectation, waiting for me to carry her round the garden. If anyone else approached her, she'd kick and howl, but when I bent over her and wrapped her up, she'd relax with a complacent sigh.

She'd object if we circled the garden in the wrong direction or followed a different path, the morning routine had to be as immutable to the child as the daily movements of the sun. We had to visit the same corners, too, the same plants and roses, which she'd lick with a tongue the size of a train-guard's flag.

Portraits I have of her, a little later, as her curled hair grew, are almost Beethovenesque in their towering passions; a series of glowering glances sweeping the room, puffs of fury, rebellion, despair, suddenly melting into sly beams of humour and outstretched, reaching love.

What were these frenzies, furies and disordered affections that accompanied her tropical growth, so rapidly developing that I could watch their day-to-day changes? Certainly I learnt to accept and attempt to guide them – the loud ill-temper, the shouting good spirits, and the overwhelming attacks of love, the biting, squeezing, tugging and thumping, the twisting of clothes and fingers. I couldn't walk beside her down the lane without being half-crippled with kicks and kisses.

How does one re-explore those earliest memories, those faded snapshots shut away in a drawer? In an old diary I dug out the other day I found a

whole series of references to the child's first fumbling months, and as an example of a father's – any father's – devotion to such trivialities, I include a selection of these below:

She sits bald and upright in her pram, watching me move about the garden. Solemn, regarding, concerned, almost critical. When she catches my eye, she gives me a quick reassuring smile.

Perhaps happiest at this time lying on her stomach on the floor, she doesn't crawl properly yet. She raises her legs and arms till all her weight's on her 'belly. Then spins round on it like a Chinese bowl.

Coming into the kitchen one morning, having for a moment forgotten her existence, I am startled to see this tough little eight-month-old figure, perched in her high arm-chair, watching me thoughtfully, kindly, and puffing on one of my pipes.

I give her a doll to play with, sitting it near her on the floor. It's dressed in a lace frock, lace bonnet and stockings, a virginal Victorian original. She reaches for its feet, and bites them.

Today I place her on the bed with some beads just out of her reach. She puts down her head, heaves up her bottom, digs in her knees, and with a squealing thrust of her body dives forward and grabs the beads. The first moment of her independence, the first step of her leaving home.

Sometimes when I see her spread idly on the sofa, I lean over and kiss her toes. She slumps back, eyes half-closed, a fat smile on her face, her mouth moving in voluptuous bliss. All is windy sighing and stillness, till I draw away. Then comes that desolate cry of desertion I know so well.

Her face changes like a beauty whose beauty changes with her mood – washed-out, pinched, screwed-up, bored and vacant, then suddenly enlivened by a quick-glowing summer radiance. Sometimes there's a soft, almost maternal tenderness in her eyes, meeting mine, a lingering faintly mocking affection. Then a storm-wrack of fury runs over her face, a fury so impersonal and overwhelming, but so illogical and unprovoked at the time, it seems to be stirred by memories of some prenatal pain or ancestral atrocity.

It is her first summer on earth and we have a series of long sunny days. We take picnics up the school-bank to a high grassy hollow which overlooks the valley.

Cathy brings a flask of tea, some biscuits, and Jessy in a sling. J. sits in the grass, tugging at flowers and swiping at butterflies. A warm breeze climbs up the bank and moves the grasses and J. slaps her bare legs and shouts with pleasure. Happy, squealing, smiling at everything now she kisses the ground, the biscuits, the cups and saucers, then rolls over and kisses her feet. She loves the big village boys on their way home from school and sighs with rapture at the sight of them.

I go to France for a few weeks and when I come back I see the bronze lusty change in the girl. She has grown more hair, the gold curls spreading, face ripening, eyes and mouth enlarging. She takes off my glasses, feeds me with chocolate, looks closely and solemnly into my face, then leans forward and gives me a series of long wet kisses, and bites me sharply on the lower lip.

A special day today. Though still only crawling, she found her way up the steep staircase alone. Puffing and clawing, and groaning, 'Oh, deah!', using her

toes and knees like a mountaineer. Arrived at the top at last with a surprised grin of fright and triumph. Then toppled all the way down again, but without real hurt, rolling slackly, over and over, like a great white pillow, slowly from stair to stair.

Late summer afternoon. I carry her in a bag on my back, down the field, across the stream and up to the hill with its view of Wales. The grass is blowing with blue and red butterflies and snapping with vetch-pods uncurled by the heat. She bubbles with happiness as I carry her along, singing hoarsely and banging me across the head.

Another perfect day. I leave my writing room in Stroud and am met at the village bus-stop by mother and daughter with a picnic basket. We go up to Bulls' Cross at the end of the valley and sit on an ancient tump overlooking Painswick. Jessy settles amiably, punches the grass, shouts, and eats everybody's sandwiches; then slowly, like a pink terrapin, crawls over her mother's body and nuzzles her face with heavy sighs and kisses.

Took her today to see Auntie Alice in Sheepscombe. Auntie cuddles her fiercely, then bounces her on her knee. Unused to such pleasantries from a virtual stranger, Jessy wriggles and protests loudly. Auntie Alice hands her back to her mother. 'I can't master her,' she says. 'She has a will. Plump, yes – but her flesh is well bestowed.'

Thirteen months. Understanding now a wide range of phrases. I'm still met, when I enter the room, by that tolerant smile, or coy hiding of the face, or a sudden rush of bull-charges across the floor with her head butting against my feet.

Sometimes yielding and romantic, lifted and held in my arms as we dance round and round the room, her warmth turning with mine, her face washed with bliss, head and shoulders leaning back in a graceful swoon, begging me huskily not to stop, and glancing with insane pride and self-consciousness, out of the corner of her eyes, to see that her mother is watching.

Generally two moods, equally extreme. Love for everything, kissing stuffed birds, the cat, lampshades, even the floor. If angry she beats her head on the wall; and if I forbid her to do something, she slaps my hand sharply and then in a moment presses it to her lips.

Still at her best going to bed. Romping wildly for the last quarter of an hour. Monkey-jumping at the rails, or scurrying up and down on all fours, sleek in her nightdress, like a silver fox. At last lying on her back, frozen, holding her breath and staring at me with that old, original look of carnality, waiting for me to buss or tickle her feet. Receives my goodnights with sharp animal yelps, then later with deep grave sighs. The teasing eyes cloud over and darken, and sleep comes smoothly and suddenly, like the moon going behind a hill.

After these first fond infant recollections of her, when she was almost a passive plaything, I watched her suddenly take over the power and growth of herself, become a thing of bouncing beauty, of ringing gaiety, of bellowing tempers

and passions, throttling her dolls and pets in spasms of uncontrolled love, commanding the world to suit her needs, the rain to stop at her word, skies to clear at a glance, that all toyshops should open on Sundays for her, and driving her will like the prow of a battleship between reality and her greedy dreams.

Following upon my quiet twelve years of marriage to her mother, her growing occupation of my life became a punitive force, expressed in daylong tyrannies, demands and disciplines, arranging my capitulations with invincible charm. Watching her, I remember her uncontrolled limbs and hair suddenly calmed by unexpected order. And she watching her mother with scornful pride, aware that they were both beauties, rivals, but sanctuaries; so that they would cling together silently for long minutes at a time, cheeks close, reflecting each other's bloom, and I'd sense the piercing brevity of the moment, that I was seeing them thus for perhaps the last time ever.

Then, suddenly, the little crawling, bawling gold-haired lump I remembered, was sixteen years old, and as tall as I was. The tiny bruised plum she had been at the beginning had filled out into a rich round fruit, as warm as noon, and centred with an indestructible diamond stone.

Almost nothing that I expected had happened between us, but a father's expectations are not of his daughter's world. I think I'd looked for a shy wisp of Colettesque sensitivity, moving with graceful adoration around me, seeking my advice, listening to my illuminations, and perhaps soothing me in the evening with a Chopin nocturne.

But as she'd grown as a daughter, so I'd grown as a father, and learnt to bury away my wishful images of her, and to watch her take charge, naturally enough, of her own directions and to develop her own independence and will.

So what I'd got now was not the compliant doll of a father's fancy, but a glowing girl with a dazzling and complicated personality, one with immense energy in chasing both happiness and despair, and who expressed her love for me, as always, not in secret half-smiles and the sharing of silences, but in noisy shouts, jolly punches, sharp jabs to the stomach, and a lively burying of teeth in arms and earlobes.

Certainly she had become no dad's soft shadow, nor ever would be now. She was existing on a different scale to my first fond imaginings. She had become herself – a normal jeans-clad, horse-riding, pop-swinging, guitar-bashing adolescent with a huge appetite for the lustier pleasures of life.

Not at all what I planned or what I expected, but I know I didn't wish her changed. Like a slap

in the face with a fresh-picked rose she was a rousing and awakening reality. She'd learnt to command the instant attention of one's eyes and ears with all the attack of a circus band. She'd become a billowing extrovert who swept through our rooms and lives with a full-throated razzama-tazz, so that with her entrances all independent activity ceased as though the windows had just blown in.

I don't think I ever knew what it was to sit in a state of relaxed quietness with her, just to be aware of her being there. Music, for her, was a thing for singing and dancing to, television for taking part in, books for throwing, pictures for knocking askew, conversation for interruption and argument.

Even when sleeping, the experience seemed

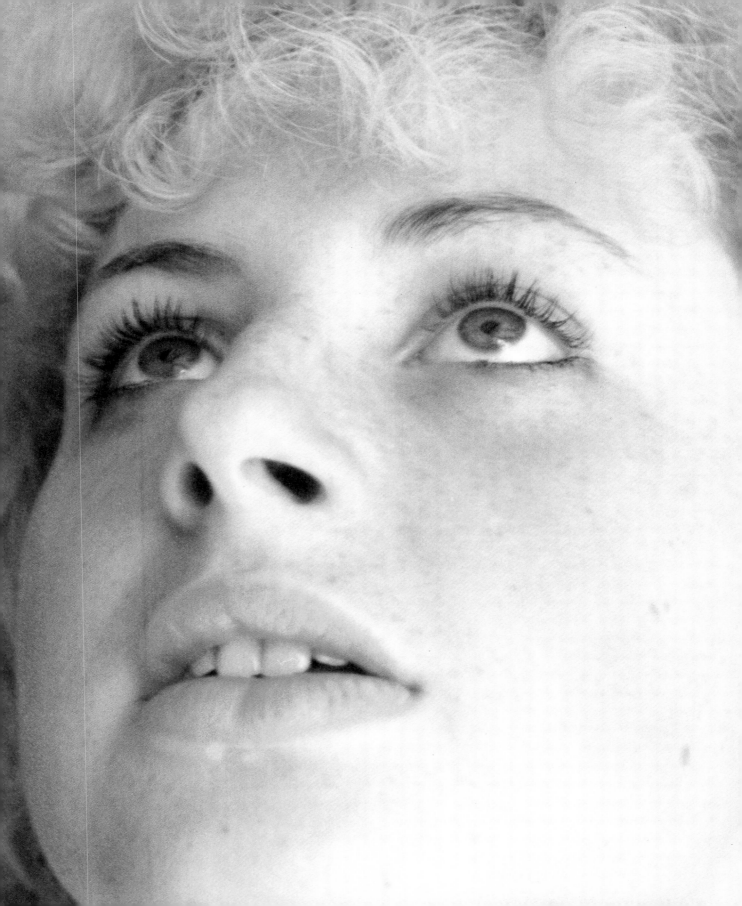

to fill her room with such storms of tossings and heavings, such a nautical flapping of sheets, one wondered how ever she got her rest. But she had become the most exciting thing to have happened to me, and I believed her very forces kept me alive.

She was now full-grown and her burning countenance magnified what that must be – a dazzling time of swirling currents and passions, of tricks with clothes and combs and mirrors, of dreams of muscled young men moving godlike through the streets, where every false word or footstep could mean disaster.

In many ways she had also become a conventional girl, as indeed most young girls must be, passing through all the chrysalis stages of growing-up to reach this golden wing-stretched moment.

First there were the dolls, kittens, galloping hamsters, circling goldfish, the budgies, and of course the horse. Accompanied, and in parallel, by an early taste for blood and horror, for crocodiles, sharks, and scarlet-fanged Draculas, with personally-signed photographs of Christopher Lee.

Later, in strict order, followed the electronic ravishers of the scenes – the brushed dolly Beatles, hamster-toothed Osmonds, Starsky and Hutch, and on to the more adult sophistications of Mike Oldfield and David Bowie. Unremarkable transitions for a growing girl, with strong appetites and uncomplicated dreams.

But how can I describe her now in her full late teens, having slipped from me into the arms of a wider world? She is beautiful without doubt, with flaring curled hair, heavy lips and a complexion

as rare as her mother's. She has all the vitality of a sunburst, volcanic passions, a voice of protean command and bubbling southsea enthusiasms.

She is never sure of the ripeness of her plans, nor or their chances to come about; indeed she often forgets them on the brink of completion. Yet she is not one, I would say, who cares to preface action with words. She hates to be alone but has a paradoxical need for independence. She treats her horse and her friends with the same rough-handed affection but seems to forget them when

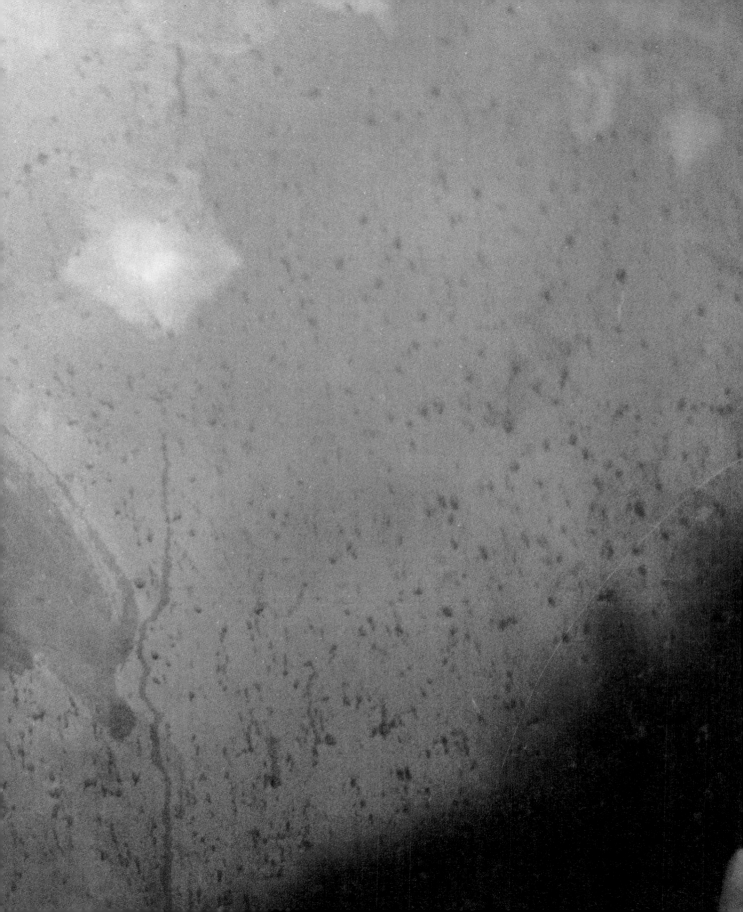

they are out of her sight. She has a generous sense of humour and accepts one's feeblest jokes with a roaring lioness's laugh of approval.

But for all her gaiety and gliding high spirits she can plunge suddenly down in unfathomable despair, and will withdraw into some close-shuttered cell to ask the walls for the truth of herself, without wishing to know the answer.

She is, I must confess, my most jealously-guarded obsession, and the late compelling spark in my life. I have spoilt her, no doubt, and overloaded her with expectations, most of which must have proved hard to bear.

But she has taught me more about women than I have learnt in a lifetime's devoted interest in the subject. The power to bruise and heal in one smooth-running sentence; to look blankly through you, then elect you king of the month. I have also had to learn to order, placate, encourage, disentangle and calm this one more than any other.

For in her I have watched the makings of a woman, year by year, almost day by day; from that plump breathing bundle first held in my arms to this assured beauty now standing shoulder to shoulder beside me.

She has also taught me some half-forgotten, primitive truths about love – that love can be an unchosen, sometimes unwanted, fact of existence, which neither moods, exasperation, nor even occasional flashes of actual dislike can alter.

For me, it is a love of both pride and compassion, a need to protect and guide, something for which I must endure, listen to lies, admit deceptions, forgive, stand waiting in the rain, or even kill.

My daughter is now playing out her closing scenes for me. The other evening I watched her dancing at home to the gramophone – something she'd done since she was small, but never quite like this. I watched a swirling figure, wrapped in a solitary glow, dancing in loose-limbed controlled abandon; dancing for her reflection in the mirror, for a glance from me; but also for that other one, unknown and unguessed at yet, for whom these spells were cast, for that future-one who must in time replace me.

And watching her dancing there in that brief and questioning solitude of her body, I felt all the sad enchantment of seeing something about to take wing. That as soon as the limbs were tested and proved, the will found to be strong enough, she would be risen and away and gone from me at last, leaving behind the dropped dolls, the circling goldfish, the empty hamster cage, and the horse in the field with its turned raised head.

Mother and daughter, nearer together now and more alike than they know, have balanced the greater part of my recent years. Easy to love such clamouring, hungry and beautiful assailants; not so easy to remain unscathed. By crowding my days, and stealing my sleep, they have also lengthened my life.

All love lives by slowly moving towards its end, and is sharpened by the snake-bite of farewell within it. The birth of my child was a farewell to the child-bride who bore her. And my daughter, now grown, must be another farewell. Perhaps I have lost both of them now, as time withdraws them from me. But the pictures in this book may hold them for a short while longer. ❧